CULTURAL GENOCIDE

GLUE AND SPY
Included

S. E. McKenzie

DEDICATION
To everyone who has been left out in the cold

TABLE OF CONTENTS

Cultural Genocide

CULTURAL GENOCIDE
I

There was nowhere
For Chee to hide
Dee Stole her pride

For Chee loved Dee
Dee did not feel the same
Cultural Genocide

Psychic Suicide

No use for guns and knives
When fear and beer
Can just as easily ruin lives.

There are bars that can bind you;
Bars that confine you;
They even have bars of love

Full of hate
Bars that trap; control fate;
Contained too much distraction

Chee remembered her True Love too late.

CULTURAL GENOCIDE: Glue and Spy Included

The music got her heart pounding
She felt feelings she never felt before
And just wanted more

The pleasure
Grew to be astounding
Before she fell to the floor

An illusion
Of make believe
Stole the innocence to cry for

Lost life
To die for
The war that never used a gun

Chee thought it would be fun
But her true love was not there
The only one who would ever care

Chee awoke in a brain drain
Now the ancient chain
Linked Chee to the system

Cultural Genocide
The pain
Caused Chee's Psychic Suicide.

One side takes all
Trying to integrate
Led to Chee's fall

No one cared or heard her scream
For her true love was not there
Too far away; in another land

Not even close to hold her hand;
And what was left of love was forgotten
Chee's Hopelessness felt too rotten

Lost identity
Took over her mind
How could Chee really see

That Dee had grown unkind

You can't go far
If you don't know
Who you are

CULTURAL GENOCIDE: Glue and Spy Included

A dirty way to fight
Which turned Chee's world
Upside down

Cultural Genocide
Progressed as Dee spoke
With a forked tongue

Hurt Chee more
Than any
Gun

II

Chee tried too hard
As each door slammed in her face
No one wanted to see her in any place

Chcc tried so hard
Just to smile
While the well to do

Looked right through Chee
As if she wasn't there
And Chee's Pain just grew.

The only thing free for Chee
Was beer; a gift from someone perverse
Then things only got worse

III

How can anyone look away during the overkill
While the underfed
Are dying in all this greed.

While they bulldoze
Affordable housing
All over town

Nowhere to grow
Many abandoned tomorrow
Lost in fear and sorrow

Nowhere to belong
Nowhere to eat
To grow strong

Too easy to feel defeat.

CULTURAL GENOCIDE: Glue and Spy Included

Cultural Genocide
Psychic Suicide
Lost pride

Nowhere to hide
Such a fine line
That keeps one sane

Fine line to block the pain
Fine like between the Haves and Have Nots
Fine line too easily broken

Then the pain will be awoken
Fine line; do not cross;
For the fine line is the boss

The line Chee was not allowed to cross
Nowhere to belong
Nowhere to eat

Chee felt defeat
Chee hoped for love
But they sexualized her

She looked for hope
But all they gave her
Were false leads and rope

In a fool's game
Where no one bleeds
Out in the open

Very few
Remember Chee's name
Most treat with disdain

Cultural Genocide
Psychic Suicide
Chee wanted to belong

They all said that she was wrong

The man wearing the boots
Told Chee to move along
Brought a tear to her eye

CULTURAL GENOCIDE: Glue and Spy Included

Chee wondered if it was better just to die

The current in the wire was moving higher
And when Chee climbed to the top
The wire cut her

Barbed and so sharp
Broken flesh could only bleed
And weaken Chee

IV

Lee started a business hoping to thrive
Soon the building fell apart
Stu's indifference broke Lee's heart.

A bird made a nest
In the hole in the wall
And sang a song to soothe Lee's mind

While the world turned an eye
The bird remembered the parking lot
As a meadow so green

Now full of cars; the beauty could not be seen.

Parking for an hour or two was all that was allowed
The attendant wouldn't be back
For the rest of the day

So all those cars were allowed to stay.

Lee saw the attendant after five
He congratulated Lee
For keeping his business alive

In the climate of cultural genocide
Lee borrowed as much money as anyone can
Hoping to have the same chance

As any other man;
Then what should appear
A no entry sign and just more fear;

As debt accumulated;
Barriers just denigrated
And divided the town

Between the Haves and Have Nots
It had always been that way
They say

CULTURAL GENOCIDE: Glue and Spy Included

Rich get richer
As the poor get poorer
Cultural Genocide

Affordable housing
Was bulldozed away
For those shacks were in the way

They were blocking the view
For the well to do
In a place were only few could belong

Chee tried to be strong
They said she was wrong
When Chee was just trying too get along

V

They bow to the thing
And all the power that money can bring
But heaven help the ones called Lee and Chee

Without a penny to their name
They will be the ones to blame
Where they stand will grow into a frame

Hate mongering
Fear mongering
With nowhere to hide

Cultural Genocide
Psychic Suicide
Lost in a world

That could be undone
If we stood as one
All together; under one sun;

That spherical flaming entity
Way up there
Power for all to share

Anchored so diligently
In the sky
Hope gave courage

So Lee and Chee gave it another try

CULTURAL GENOCIDE: Glue and Spy Included

As they stood below
Fusion power so mighty
They hoped to grow

A better tomorrow
For the sun
Was beginning to shine

And a day had just begun

Blinding to the naked eye
Divine Hotness on show
So much we will never know

The Sun brought life
While water fed it
During all of this misery

Blessed; ancient; mystery.

So you and I, could grow
In Paradise not really lost
Just behind a golden gate

Controls fate
Stirs up hate
Cultural Genocide

Psychic Suicide

The mightiest power of all
One day will be
Pure balance would soon reclaim

And will know Chee and Lee's name
Then all would be well
Once Lee and Chee escaped this Hell.

THE END

GLUE

GLUE
I

The Bubble was about to pop
The bottom was about to drop
The clock was about to stop

Lines were forming
The air was warming
The Ozone level was rising

The whole world appeared to be uprising;

The Bubble overvalued things
The trouble had just begun
The rubble was everywhere

For Money Front-runners
Had swept the land;
We were all under Storm-Man's command.

We tried not to forget the power of our love
For it was stronger than any glue;
Brighter than any star

CULTURAL GENOCIDE: Glue and Spy Included

Far above every war
Could heal the deepest scar
Would defy those willing to lie.

We walked by a long line
Outside the Money Mart.
Rolling out stuff

In a grocery cart
It was a bad start
And our future was up in air

So much wasn't fair.

Gated; Poverty so legislated
Too little measured;
Too much speculated;

Branded; all we had was our True Love.

Our Love would try to unify;
And free us from bias
Negative response loop;

Storm-Man's negative pull;
Was said to be the new social science
Zero tolerance for defiance;

For Storm-Man was a political predator
Social Speculator
And ruled with an iron fist;

While the list of the missing debtors grew.

Storm-Man's blood lust was showing
With gun in hand he manufactured our consent
We heard many had been buried in cement.

Storm-Man told us how to live;
And told Momma
When to die;

We knew the power of our Love was true;
For it was brighter than any star;
Far above every war;

Would heal the deepest scar.

CULTURAL GENOCIDE: Glue and Spy Included

II
True love
Mending in unity
True Love giving us new opportunity;

Empowering every community;
Even when Faded Brown Shirted Storm-Man
Appeared from the past.

The Money Front-runners were in charge

While a positive feed-back loop
Took a life of its own
While Storm-Man

Political Predator;
Another social speculator
Touched every debtor

With their heart of stone.

Storm-Man was protected by Impunity
Culture of Obstruction
To displace Opportunity.

Nasty Devolution
Pushing; Shoving;
Never loving

Told us where to stand
While we waited
They looked at us as if we were hated

Gated in poverty that was legislated
Too little measured;
Too much was speculated;

While the Bubble was bursting
Many of us were hurting
Even though we knew

True Love would get us through
For it was brighter than any star
Far above every war

Could heal every scar
That was branding us
In unforgiving bias

CULTURAL GENOCIDE: Glue and Spy Included

Nasty Devolution

Culture of Obstruction
Like Glue
Kept us stuck to the past;

Political Predator
Social Speculator
Holding us back

Refusing to hear

Trapped in a culture of fear;
Just another invisible hand
Manipulating supply and demand

Across the land.

Gated by Legislated Poverty
And Hatred
Too little measured

Too much speculated;
Sheltered by Impunity
Storm-Man; political predator

From the past
Had returned
Many dropped dead before they had learned;

Lost Opportunity

Nasty Devolution
While we knew True Love
Was the only cure;

For True Love would always shine
Brighter than any star
Far above every war

Could heal the deepest scar.

And we knew
Safety was in our Unity;
And True Love would find a way;

To energize us;
Keep us strong
While the world was going wrong.

CULTURAL GENOCIDE: Glue and Spy Included

The Bubble was bursting
Opening the floor
As value sunk into the bottomless pit

Some called the Abyss
Others called it
An Opportunity missed.

As Storm-Man
Was empowered by the Devolution
He could put us in a slot;

He could order us to be shot;

Nasty Devolution
Shaped who we could be
While Storm-Man was granted Impunity

We had all our stuff
In a grocery cart
Walking past lines at the Money Mart
Our True Love would always shine

Brighter than any star
Far above every war
Would heal the deepest scar

As Culture of Obstruction got in the way
Made us miss
Another Opportunity.

III

Faded Brown Shirted Storm-Man

Political Predator
Social Speculator
Was kicking his boots

Stared and glared with bias which was oozing
We had all of our stuff in a shopping cart
Went by a long line

Outside the Money Mart
Then we hid in the park
Once it was dark

CULTURAL GENOCIDE: Glue and Spy Included

Mind Shaker
Grave Digger
Goal Breaker

For a few hundred dollars an hour
Gated Legislated Poverty
Made us feel hated

While the Bubble was getting ready to burst.

IV
We hold on
To our dream
Of True love

So we have something to believe in
Which is brighter than any star
Far above every war

Where opposite sides are seen no more.
In reality we fight to survive.
We were put on a list

Said we were missing
Though we were behind that Tree
Hiding from Storm-Man

With all our stuff
In a grocery cart
As the line outside the Money Mart

Was growing
As the Bubble was bursting in spurts
We knew many would be getting hurt.

We could not speak out, we were not free,
Did not want to be taken away
To a place where we would have no say.

We knew our capture would create a good job for the few;
For the rest of us
We dreamed of a love that would be true.

CULTURAL GENOCIDE: Glue and Spy Included

A love that would unite us
Not force us to fight
For our rights under bias

While the Bubble was so inflated
It was about to pop
And the clock was about to stop

Many would go mad
And jump from their roof top
Many would be left newly poor

While Storm-Man would be in his domain

As the bottom of the market sank
The Abyss came to light
Gave many a terrible fright

And we saw it all

As we hid behind that Holy Tree
Storm-Man could not see
Where we were

You know the Tree

That lived through
Different times of war
As it grew

We knew
True Love would never die
For it was brighter than any star

Far above every war
Could heal the deepest scar
After Storm-Man had his way.

Took over our ground
Nasty Devolution
True Love was the only solution;

Our hope
Was said to be
Mind pollution.

Turned Love into a bad word
So we called Love God
Because Hate was growing into the Destroyer.

CULTURAL GENOCIDE: Glue and Spy Included

Birth and decay
Luck and the unknown
Needed some Magical Thinking.
V
Storm-Man
Protected by Impunity;
Toxifying our Opportunity

Showing off his Hypocrisy

Feeling more important than you and me;
Tripping over his power lacking legitimacy
Before the fall

A list was made
Of debtors gone missing
But we were hiding behind that Tree

We all knew where we were;
The Faded Brown Shirted Storm-Man
Would try to break our bond in two

But we knew the power
Of our Love was true
It was mightier than glue

And could not be broken;
For we knew our True Love
Would shine brighter than any star

Far above every war;
Would heal
The deepest scar.

Our True Love would be always mending;
Our hurt inside kept us bending;
As we hung our heads low.

Storm-Man
Ordered us about
Sounded like a drone;

He knew we were alone

His droning was Mind numbing
And he was slow
That is why we kept low.

VI

The boom was good
For many; it was true;
The Frenzy felt so right

As the Bubble inflated
And grew
Around me and you

Some said the Bubble
Would burst suddenly
Which was why Storm-Man

Brought fear here;
Arrived so fast;
He was summoned from the past;

He would have watched us all day
But that Tree was in the way
And Bird sang so happily

For new life just hatched that was family.
While the Bubble was bursting
We saw many lining up by the banks

S.E. McKENZIE

Nasty Devolution
Political Predator
Social Speculator

Down to a science
Zero tolerance for defiance
As the Money Front-runners

Touched every debtor

With their heart of stone.
As we searched
For opportunity we felt so alone.

As we pushed all of our stuff in a grocery cart
We went by the long line
Outside the Money Mart

Storm-Man
Was standing in our way
While we were stereotyped

CULTURAL GENOCIDE: Glue and Spy Included

In hype for his force of external greed
We would not be weakened by our need
For we had our True Love by our side.

The cost of the Bubble bursting was out of sight
We knew our True Love
Was meant to unite

While Storm-Man

Sold what he could;
Sad man;
Weak man;

Never knew
What the power
Of love could do.

For he was a Liquidator
Just another Hater
For Profit.

The Bubble was bursting
Pushed prices through the floor
And into the Abyss

The bank was closed, the CEO had locked the door.

As the Bubble was bursting
Storm-Man yelled and screamed
He was protecting someone's revenue stream

Before he pushed some of us into his bottomless pit.

And True Love
Would link us hand in hand
All across

Our Mother Land

And Free us
From Storm-Man's Pull
As the Bubble was bursting all around.

VII

We knew
Our Love so true
Would get us through

The lies.
We knew our Love would energize
Grow into a great Power to behold

The new gold.
And we knew our love would
Show us the way.

Storm-Man
Was very angry indeed
For his hunger left him in constant need.

While the Bubble was bursting
He was frowning; pounding;
While we waited for the clock to stop ticking.

The floor above the abyss began to drop
Storm-Man demanded more profit
As many more were pushed into the bottomless pit.

Storm-Man was no longer lost in time;
He screamed,
He was still heartless and mean;

Overvalued assets
Made many feel richer than they were
Which inflated the Bubble even more

As competition was ran out of town;

They left silently, never causing a scene.
For Storm-Man
Was a weak man

A sad man

Lost his faith a long time ago
In Love so True
His heart grew bitter.

CULTURAL GENOCIDE: Glue and Spy Included

And we all knew
True Love was brighter than any star
Far above every war;

Could heal the deepest scar.
Would end oppression
Turn around negative suggestion.

Help share our common ground
Standing as one
Under one Sun

The bond of Love
Would make us one;
As we found a way to feed

Those dying in all this greed.
As the Bubble was bursting
Love would help us rise to our feet;

Would heal the deepest scar.

Storm-Man
Was so afraid of those he persecuted
He demanded them to be executed.

Prejudicial, No need for magical thinking

Storm-Man preferred to get us
Mindlessly drinking
For he needed us weaker than he

So he could manufacture
Our consent more freely
In this world; some called Paradise Lost

The true opportunity cost.

VIII

True Love was real
Willing and able,
To be as strong as love could be;

CULTURAL GENOCIDE: Glue and Spy Included

Unifying loose ends;
Needing no amends;
Glued in True Love;

We were meant to unify then die.

Love was a giant jar of glue;
Power; when no one knew what to do;
A flower; blooming where ever it can

As trust bound the Rights of Man
Broken in war
Broken pieces all over the floor

Sinking into the Abyss
As the Bubble was breaking
The ground was shaking.

Trust glued some bonds back together again
The bonds were strong
Held us together for times so long.

Glued as one
One world, one life
While Storm-Man demanded a Negative Response Loop

S.E. McKENZIE

Demanded more strife.

IX

We grow at life in trust
For we must
Dream

Today is the bridge
Between Yesterday and Tomorrow
Elevating and bonding

Ending all sorrow
True Love was the glue
That we knew would bond us as one.

Storm-Man tried to put an end
To our positive response loop;
Storm-Man wanted control.

He wanted his negative loop to dominate
Would cause hate
To vibrate.

He would smile while
Impunity paid the bill;
For the Faded Brown Shirted Storm-Man

S.E. McKENZIE

Demanded more strife.

IX

We grow at life in trust
For we must
Dream

Today is the bridge
Between Yesterday and Tomorrow
Elevating and bonding

Ending all sorrow
True Love was the glue
That we knew would bond us as one.

Storm-Man tried to put an end
To our positive response loop;
Storm-Man wanted control.

He wanted his negative loop to dominate
Would cause hate
To vibrate.

He would smile while
Impunity paid the bill;
For the Faded Brown Shirted Storm-Man

CULTURAL GENOCIDE: Glue and Spy Included

Was a liquidator
Just another hater
Waiting for the day

The Bubble would burst;
Out of sight
The floor above the Abyss

Would drop

Old rulers die hard;
Death was only days away;
And we knew our True Love

Was brighter than any star;
Far beyond every war;
Would heal the deepest scar.

A better destiny for sure
True Love was the only cure.
The Glue to bond us as one

Under one Sun.

X

True Love was forgotten
Not by us
But by those who had everything money could buy;

And needed nothing more
As the Bubble was bursting
The Abyss had opened its floor.

Deep below
Was the bottomless pit
So the ones thrown in could fit.

The Liquidator
Social Speculator
Touched every debtor

With their heart of stone.

While shedding crocodile tears;
Never looking at us
In the eye.

CULTURAL GENOCIDE: Glue and Spy Included

"And without True Love
All the hurt could not be forgotten,"
Hope cried out again.

Storm-Man
Will fool them again!
While they look away

Many will be pushed into the Bottomless Pit
As the Abyss
Opens the door.

Another Liquidation
Another hurt sensation
Watching Storm-Man scream
Our dream away

So many pushed
Into the other side;
Making money feeds Storm-Man's pride;

Storm-Man will tell them how to live;
And tell their Momma when to die;
He will turn away when they cry.

Just another war crime
Before our time;
The ghosts of yesterday wanted to stay."

True Love replied to Hope;
"Yes, I will make you stronger
Then it will be easier to cope."

"I know you, True Love,
Will do what you can
But how do you soften

Faded Brown Shirted Storm-Man?
Another liquidator;
Waiting for the Floor to drop

Just another hater, another goal breaker;
Pushing who he can into
The Bottomless Pit."

And True Love replied
"We have you, Hope,
And you strengthen me.

CULTURAL GENOCIDE: Glue and Spy Included

As long as I have you, I shall never die."
Hope replied.
"Some say

True Love is the road to suicide.

But we know the opposite is true;
We know what we must do
To free the people from Storm-Man's reign;

We must unite; go beyond the pain;
Love and Hope, together, so electrifying;
Before the Bubble bursts.

How do we forgive Storm-Man?
He defames who he can.
We knew our true love would find a way.

We knew our True Love
Was brighter than any star
Far above every war

Would heal the deepest scar.

And we knew too
Hope and True Love
Would unite.

Showed us strength
We never knew we had;
And then we felt no fear;

So we didn't feel so sad.
We were able to forgive
And our strength grew

That was when we knew
That the power of Love was really true
And was deep in our hearts

Buried in the dark
While we slept in the park
As the Faded Brown Shirted Storm-Man

Militarized everything in sight
Belted out his might
Caused us a terrible fright.

XI

Storm-Man
Had a billing code slot
For everything that wasn't shot

Hope waited Her turn
Then held True Love's hand.
"Yes I know all about You

You, so True, you are my Inspiration.
Mystical; magical;
Ancient sensation

For the last generation
Without a home
Nowhere to roam

Shielded behind our positive response loop
Storm-Man
Pulled out his loop of negativity

We could feel it drone
It was so near
We felt so much fear.

We tried to stand up for what was right
With enough strength and courage
To let live

But that only started a fight
That we could never win
While our True Love

Was called a sin
We knew our True Love would unite
And glow brighter than any star

Shining above every war
Healing the deepest scar
As our True Love grew

It would stay glued; stronger than tar;
As manufactured war, famine and drought;
We knew Storm-Man had too much clout.

We wanted to be free
Form his power of negativity
Starvation, division and confusion;

CULTURAL GENOCIDE: Glue and Spy Included

As the Bubble was bursting
We let our True Love bloom
Hoping it would take us beyond

Exclusion and doom."
True Love replied,
After she cried.

"We must never be confined
Or be a slave to any master mind
For the world needs us now

More than ever before.

For we,
You and me
Hope and Love,

Work best as one
Under one Sun
Stronger than glue.

Working together
For millennia
Stronger than any militia

.

Though we know
We better grow faster,"
Hope said with a sigh;

"I see the new age of hysteria
Arriving as the Bubble is bursting."
Hope tried not to cry.

XII

Love and Hope glued us as one
Connecting and mending
Love and Hope were spread all around;

Divided no more;

Found common ground;
Felt our mass heart pound;
The skin drum sent signals of sound;

Yes it is true
We were alive
We had survived

As we could hear the echoes

CULTURAL GENOCIDE: Glue and Spy Included

Of the overkilling
Of the underfed
Storm-Man found it thrilling.

Love would mend broken hearts
That were torn apart
And make them whole again

Love would bond stronger than glue
Make us as one
Under one Sun

That shines so bright
When no clouds are in the way
Regardless of what was done that day.

Love's Bond could glue
And mend every heart
That had been torn apart

For we knew
That Love so True
Was brighter than any star

Far above every war
Would heal the deepest scar."
And Hope agreed.

I hugged the Tree
So near to me
And hoped

The Faded Brown Shirted Storm-Man
Did not see
For I needed a good vibration

To face the world that day.

XIII

We are born into this world
So broken and torn;
Only Love's glue could help it mend

Show us when to bend;
While Storm-Man
Militarized and liquidated

All he could;
Things began to rust;
And there was a loss of human trust;

It was true; we felt hated.

CULTURAL GENOCIDE: Glue and Spy Included

We knew it was getting late
And fate was around the bend
We needed to mend.

Broken lines were everywhere
So many; we didn't care.
Some lines were manufactured to divide us;

Some just to antagonize us;
We had plenty of reason to hide
As we held on to the Tree.

The Bubble was bursting
The bottom had opened into a bottomless pit
And nothing could be free

We knew our love so true was the only way
For it was brighter than any star
Far above ever war

And would heal the deepest scar.

Our feet were free to roam;
And we knew we might never have a home;
Living our days misunderstood;

We were rejected
And now free
To raise the pillars

In a dark world of killers
Our pillars absorbed the shock
We grew; for we were still young;

And we were
To build the new world
That was promised a long time ago.

For we had the Glue
And the First Pillar
Was absorbing the shock.

"We gave it all that we got,"
Hope and Love said at once
Storm-Man was clicking his boots.

CULTURAL GENOCIDE: Glue and Spy Included

XIV

We were running out of time;
We had witnessed Storm-Man's crime;
We had a long way to climb;

For Devolution; manufactured consent;
Left many buried in cement;
And many more were pushed into the bottomless pit

As the Bubble was bursting.

While Storm-Man
Was liquidating and intimidating;
We all ran away.

XV

While we were coping;
And saving
Whatever we could.

We did not know
The many who were shot;
We knew there had been a lot.

The Macro Power
Over-lorded the Micro
Even though Micro was the core;

The Bubble was still bursting

XV

Micro and the Macro were one
Needed glue;
For the world was so broken;

And could have been whole
As one
Under One Sun

And the implosion
Opened the floor
Just like before

And many were pushed into the pit;
Liquidated, intimidated;
We knew there was a better way.

We found the strength to forgive;
And did the best
We could to live;

For we knew
What True Love could do;
It was brighter than any star;

Far above every war
Light enough
To heal the deepest scar

Made us one
Under one Sun
As the building of the new world

Had just begun.

THE END

S.E. McKENZIE

SPY

CULTURAL GENOCIDE: Glue and Spy Included

SPY
I

Some said they had to forgive
So they could let some joy live
Under the setting sun

Glowing over
Failed City
Still so pretty

In the morning sun too
Many were poor
But didn't feel blue

Their time had not yet come to an end
So the persecuted rose to their feet
Always staying on their side of the street

Not yet polluted, the mouth of the mighty river
Welcomed larvae carried by ocean currents;
As time flew

The larvae grew
Into fish
Big enough to eat

Free from body politics
So confining
And mind numbing

The eagles flourished
Living in the giant trees
While the flowers nearby

Attracted honey bees.
Puffy said
"I am master to all this."

Puffy built a fence to keep
All the nature in
And the uninvited out.

The excluded didn't cry and didn't shout
Some said they had to forgive
So they could let some joy live

CULTURAL GENOCIDE: Glue and Spy Included

Under the setting sun
Glowing over
Failed City
Still so pretty

Puffy, was one of many elected officials;
Lost effectiveness; Lost legitimacy
Though no one knew for sure

What came first
The Failing City;
Or the Failing Puffy

Sat on a rock
He was in shock
Failing city

Was still so pretty

Able to defy
Common sense
Puffy did not control petty expense

So locked into rules to protect fools;

The persecuted were feared;
For they looked so hungry all the time;
Puffy declared that they were unfit to live;

And the well to do agreed
So caught they were
In their greed

To some, Fear was might,
To others Forgiveness made things right,
Everyone could agree

It would take a lot of love
To prevent
World War III

As the autocracy
And mind numbing bureaucracy
Declared that Failing City

Was the happiest place of all
Though only the well to do
Need to drop by to have a ball

CULTURAL GENOCIDE: Glue and Spy Included

Hate and Love still lived; setting passions on fire;

Puffy praised all
The wealth
That he had under his command

He kneeled before the Invisible Hand
That was said to be touching everything in the land
And was the only force that seemed to care.

Puffy wasn't self-aware
And we were on our guard
Living in separate worlds

Was the only way
We could survive
To never let them into our minds

We had two faces
The one we showed to those we owed
And our own

We were unbroken
Though our pain had awoken
We were young enough

To have a heart full of love.
The visible bopping heads projected
A world divided and unfair
As the river raged

The sun was hidden
As the rain came in torrents
And soaked into the ground

The bopping heads would not listen to warnings
That the raging river
Was eroding the dyke

In the river's bend
Even though Puffy's home
Was standing there behind the fence

To keep all the nature in
And all the uninvited out
As the river raged freely

CULTURAL GENOCIDE: Glue and Spy Included

Beyond the power of the 'Well To Do'.

Puffy said
The Dyke could be managed
For another day

And told the engineers to move on
As the 'Well To Do' continued to project
Their day away so freely

Sitting in Failing City;
The Dyke would was not built
To hold back the super-flood's raging waters

Many avoided the town
Said it was the city of doom
Decaying too fast;

As Puffy sat on his wall
The engineers predicted
That he would have a very great fall

While the collective mind of the well to do
Was living in the past;
So their autocratic power could last

We kept low
Tried not to show
Everything we know;

Projecting at will for a thrill
Words taken out of context
For a fight; they did it all night;

Too close for comfort, and too far away to communicate;
The policy function was never executed
Lost opportunity to integrate

Lost channel to communicate

Policy never lived through the day
And was buried
Under bad news

Puffy was so ineffective,
He sat on the wall
And everyone knew

CULTURAL GENOCIDE: Glue and Spy Included

That he was going to have a great fall.

Jethro and Bill were hired
To put things back together again
Failing City was broken into two parts

The 'Have Nots' and the 'Well To Do';

Lived as if there was a wall in between
When they met; they never spoke
Prevented a scene;

Some tried to smile
And were accused
Of substance abuse

As the barrier's reflection
Pushed out those
Who tried to get into the door

They were told that they weren't wanted no more.
Some had a lot
Others were doomed to be a Have Not;

Forced to live
In squalor and rot
As the 'Well To Do' claimed and framed

Within their self-serving projection
They were paid to project all day
Good Job; Good Pay;

Standing on their Pedestal
Was their favorite thing to do;
Looking down; wearing a frown;

As their neighbor's house
Was burning down;
They fought over words

In the usual way
And they had nothing much
More to say

Injury to our community
Was done on our side of the fence
We forgave; Easier to behave;

CULTURAL GENOCIDE: Glue and Spy Included

We were not broken
Still young enough
To have a heart full of love

Out of time
Out of sync
The loss was hidden in black ink

Whispers spoken not meant to be heard
By anyone like me and you
Such was the power to be elite

So entitled to stand on their feet;
We too refused to be broken;
While the fire raged;

The water tower
Had bccn sold
No one was told

We heard the whispering;
Manufactured words so decisive
If they were trying for peace

It would have been malpractice
To demoralize and criticize;
Would never break the ice

That was what Global Warming was for

We refused to be broken
We had our two faces
We knew we could survive

As long as we stayed alive
We too would stand on our feet
We too would not fade away

Or die in all this greed;

As the deer ran by; we saw them hide;
Before they were shot;
Which was done a lot;

Just like us
We were trapped on a slot
So easily shot;

CULTURAL GENOCIDE: Glue and Spy Included

Road kill by any other name
Would have been sad
And called a shame

But many could not see
Behind the fence
Built to keep the nature in

And the uninvited out
Jethro and Bill
Were having another barbecue

And the fire was very hot;

Meaning of what was said
Was relative
To how we had to live

We were silent
In ear shot
And hid

For we were unbroken
Our pain had awoken
But we had our two faces to survive

And we were so thankful to still be alive

We were still young enough
To have a heart
Full of love

What we were able to give
Was so energizing
And satisfying

More than just a voice in our head
Which was never allowed to speak
Was meant to keep us weak

Conscience was flaming before the fall
The Humpty Dumpties
Were sitting on their wall

They wanted it all;

CULTURAL GENOCIDE: Glue and Spy Included

Thought the rules
To protect fools
Could protect them

From the River's might.
The rules of fear
Made it hard to hear

The words of the engineer
Said many times before
That the riverbanks were eroding

And the dyke would not hold
The water rushing through
At the river's bend

The dyke needed to be reconstructed soon
Or the Failing City; So pretty;
Glowing under the setting sun

Was doomed
For the dyke
Would not hold

And the trees
Soaking so much water
Had been sold

The dyke could not hold
During a Super Flood
The ground would turn to mud.

And the war of words had just begun
As the Have Nots
Were pushed out of the door

No need for you to be here
You are too poor
Come back when you have more

We are still the Promised Land
Touched
By the Invisible Hand

So they could project all day
About people
Who had no say

CULTURAL GENOCIDE: Glue and Spy Included

Good Job; Good Pay;

Living in a land
That used to grow plenty
Now was running on empty

As the Early Birds flew away

We would not be broken
Though our pain had awoken
We were young enough

To have a heart full of love.

II
And how we tried
To defy all the stereotypes and lies;
Hypocrisy; too willfully blind to see;

Sometimes they knew our names;
We did not count;
We were living on the other side of the tracks;

We did not even know how to play their games;

We were Subject Material
For projecting into words
So Mystical and Prejudicial

No Entry Point
To connect into
No interface to grow

Failing City

Some of us were debtors; some of us were owed;
Many of us had nowhere to park
So we were all towed;

Making way for a bike lane
Too green to be mean
Lost under snow

Marginalized and disenfranchised
Always subject material
For projection

CULTURAL GENOCIDE: Glue and Spy Included

As Jethro and Bill
Flew above us; in the air;
Good Job; Good Pay;

We had nowhere to go
As cars were pulled into a lot beside the Money Mart
Both places always cost a lot.

As we poor, grew poorer,
The rich grew in stature;
They stood hand in hand, on their pedestal,

While Humpty Dumpty sat on his wall;
Some looked away
Knowing there would be a fall

For all the rules in the land
Could not protect such fools;
From Fate.

For Cruelty Ruled
And we knew why.
We young were kicked down

And learned not to cry
In Failing City
Broken in Two

We were the other half
Wearing the outside face
As we roamed from place to place;

There was no way back
We We knew we were spoken about behind our backs
For we were born on the wrong side
Of the Railway Track

Related by blood and that was all
And once down on our luck

We had to crawl
Through Sprawl
As our fear continued to grow

Many forgot to plan for tomorrow
Failing City, no economic viability
For it had so little virility

III

The young were run out of town
So another Humpty Dumpty could wear the crown
As he sat on his wall; he frowned;

CULTURAL GENOCIDE: Glue and Spy Included

Puffy's assistants; Jethro and Bill
Had a secret thrill
And it was to barbecue,

Sometimes in a meadow
So green,
Not often ever seen.

Where Free Spirits
Thought they could live
Until they were ready to die

While Jethro and Bill
Were flying
High in the sky

Their next biggest thrill
Was to interfere
With anyone near

And in sight
For they were in full flight
Though they would always stop

For Barbeque

S.E. McKENZIE

These surveillance men in the sky
Had many things to do
We all knew that was true;

Whenever there was a chance nearby
Jethro and Bill
Would take time off

To hunt for barbeque
A secret thrill
For Jethro and Bill

They knew when to hide from Puffy

Who ruled Failing City by fear;
Hired these surveillance men,
Hoping intelligence was always near;

Good Job; Good Pay;

CULTURAL GENOCIDE: Glue and Spy Included

To watch the mob;
From the air;
Way up there;

Jethro and Bill always found the time
To stop for Barbeque
When opportunity met their eye

So much to see
When they were
Flying high in the sky

No right to privacy
As far as we can see
In Failing City;

Too rigid to be
Fluid
Moving against the flow of time.

IV

What a thrill
For Jethro and Bill
To take photos of everything in sight

Made it harder for us to think
Let alone dream
Made some want to scream

Once our guard was down
Our vulnerability set in;
That was the time Jethro and Bill would intrude

Announcing on their one way speaker radio
That we were all rude and the 'Well To Do'
Wanted us to go;

For they blamed us for their failing town
Blamed us for bringing them down;
Some said ventilation and unfair speculation

Made good projection for all

CULTURAL GENOCIDE: Glue and Spy Included

And that was before the fall
When Humpty Dumpty fell off the wall
Jethro and Bill saw it all;

It was their role
For mind control;
Good Job; Good Pay;

Jethro and Bill
Let nothing else
Get in the way

The years went by
Some were born
And some were given permission to die

Without even asking why.

Danger was in the air
And everywhere
But Jethro and Bill

Didn't care
Too busy looking for Barbeque
While surveilling me and you.

Jethro and Bill
Were fired on the Spot
When Puffy's finances grew too hot

And Puffy was found to be

Caught up in a terrible controversy
When spending could no longer be justified
As political

Puffy tried using words that were mystical

V
Jethro and Bill's new job
Was the same as their old job
To marginalize and criticize

Sometimes in disguise

CULTURAL GENOCIDE: Glue and Spy Included

And always to survey
Made us obey
Watching so high in the sky

Good Job; Good Pay;
Never got in the way of their hunt though
For Barbeque was never too hidden

And never forbidden;

Vulnerability;
Of Momma Deer To Be
Was a fact; naturally;

She tried so hard to avoid; Human contact;

She stood still
Hoping for a higher will
To leave her unbroken

Meanwhile
Jethro and Bill loved the thrill of the kill
Remained their favorite thing to do

Equal to surveying everyone everywhere
From the air
Without a care.

Looking at us as if we had no right to be there.

As they flew in the sky
A cloud of Happy Drink
Would flow into our stream

Some started to scream
And never knew why
Then they were given permission to die.

Jethro and Bill
Knew their job well
And it was to hunt us down

And to kick us out of town

CULTURAL GENOCIDE: Glue and Spy Included

For we were the 'Have Nots'
And the price of realestate
Was about to crash

Would leave many
Without any cash
And we were blamed for Failing City

Never elected at all;
Narrow scope of vision;
Poisoned by suspicion;

Only ones allowed to make a decision;

As the eye and the pie in the sky
Were circling us from the air
We knew the line

For it too was written
From the sky
Told us what to do; everyday;

In every way;

How to live; and when to die
And what to say on the way
Manufacturing consent day by day.

As Jethro and Bill flew by
Looking for barbecue
From the sky.

And to survey
One day; to make us obey
In some degrading way;

Like you know who.
But first Jethro and Bill
Wanted the thrill of Barbecue.

VI

We never knew when
The bulldozers would come
But we knew it would be some day

We hoped many years from now.
Still we knew the bulldozers
Were on their way

CULTURAL GENOCIDE: Glue and Spy Included

While Jethro and Bill
Were having a thrill
Doing Barbeque

Waiting in line;
Every day for everything;
Life in Failed City

Was a waiting game;
Interrupted
By random cues;

Often inflating
IOUs;
Felt so dehumanizing for me and you.

We would soon be dispossessed
Were hoping that life
Could bring on the best

Soon we realized the trap
Of concrete everywhere
As Jethro and Bill

Flew in the air
Above
Nothing was about love

Jethro and Bill
Looked right through me and you
For they were hunting

For Barbecue

In the other part of town
So many
Felt so down

Waiting in soon to be Bulldozed homes
Have Nots faced the barrier of concrete unknowns
For they were just paying rent

And the plan was to sell the land
To retired folk from out of town
Who would be easy to command.

"Move in
Win win
You will love the view

CULTURAL GENOCIDE: Glue and Spy Included

So much to do;
For Jethro and Bill
Surveying in the air

Watching us
As we try to do chores
Visit the stores.

While it was getting warmer
Day by day;
So Barbeque was always on its way."

Puffy wrote a message for the nation
The speech lacked sensation
Puffy had little imagination

Though projection was his strength
He always said
And the ones who objected

Were only slaves to the voices in their collective head
Puffy said many times a day
Good job; Good Pay;

"Silence is better," that is what Puffy said;
We were denied common sense;
While his culture of obstruction; forced confusion;

So external;

Always a peril
For every living thing
Even for the rabbits

Living in the rabbit hole

Where Momma rabbit made a home
Under concrete and stone
It was her own

Her family was content
Though some called her a pest
She tried her best

To stay unbroken.

The message to bore
Was sent with great speed
So loud; could not be ignored.

Message broadcasted from the air.
People heard the word;
And thought all would be right;

Until they too were surveilled
All through the night;
Then it just didn't feel right;

But made the well to do
Feel braver
And safer.

VII

Sometimes Jethro and Bill
Would fly into Myria
To spy from the air on those living there.

To fight a force no one would name
Though it was the force
Everyone was to blame.

The genteel crowd was happy all the same
They owned their home
While the displaced

Were still free to roam

Slept all over the place
But the genteel crowd
Looked away

And summoned the list
Where complainers could meet
They loved to micro-managed that way

Good for control
Which was the role
For the eye in sky

CULTURAL GENOCIDE: Glue and Spy Included

Some say
We will die
When told; Still not too old;

Never too late
For such a fate;
Lost words; hidden in fear and hate;

Failed city
Where many were waiting
Until they were told to die.

On the other side of town
The poor were provoked
And to not to speak

They were so hungry and very weak

They phoned the authorities
To have them moved out of the way
And banned.

So they could see more land

They demanded roads
To be privatized
So only the chosen few

The 'Well To Do'
Would be entitled
To be there

Everyone else could be displaced
The 'Well To Do'
Didn't know their face

Living behind the fence
To keep all the nature in
And the uninvited out

So quick to draw conclusion
So slick they were fooled
By all the confusion

CULTURAL GENOCIDE: Glue and Spy Included

The doggy eat doggy world
Had only
Just begun

While the failed city
Glowed
Under the setting sun

Advertised
As the happiest place around
As the torrents of rain

Could no longer soak into the ground

While many more Humpty Dumpties
Sat on the wall
Looking at it all

Watching the poor and the destitute crawl
But we were not broken
We knew they were going to fall

Out of sight
Was out of mind
While Jethro and Bill

Though they could see everything from the air

As re-construction of road furniture
Had just begun
On the poor side of town

No entry signs were put up
The sort that looked like delete
The poor were so hungry they had nothing to eat

The genteel crowd
Complained
Thought those rough folk

Should be detained
While it rained
The water could not soak into the ground

For too many trees had been cut down
Taken away
And sold in town.

CULTURAL GENOCIDE: Glue and Spy Included

"The roads should be privatized,"
All the Humpty Dumpties said at once;
As they were getting ready to pounce;

Though the roads were paid for by the public purse
It was ruled by Puffy
So things just got worse

While the watchers; Jethro and Bill;
Watched us for money and thrill
Above Failing City

Below all Heavenly Bodies.
The Humpty Dumpties forced the landless to pay
For the poor and destitute had no say

The Humpty Dumpties
Had one way
And knew nothing more

They lived behind a fence
To keep the nature in
And the uninvited out.

We refused to be broken
Or to be frozen in Time.
We progressed the best we could;

Like our Papa's would;

So we all walked by
And went to the mall
Where all the merchants were renting the hall

Behind empty stores hidden
By a pretty paper wall
Puffy pointed to the crowd

As he read the rules Out loud
We knew the rules
Could not protect the fools

And we were not broken
Would not be demoralized
When criticize

CULTURAL GENOCIDE: Glue and Spy Included

For we were waiting for the fall
Never distracted
By the window dressing

In the Hall
In the Mall
Of the failing city

So pretty
When glowing
Under the setting sun.

VIII

Others asked if this should be
Government's role at all
Others were too afraid

To say anything before the Fall
And went on their way
Cherishing the silence

After filling out the form
Which was demanded of them
Whiles they could hear the hum

Of the surveillance men
Jethro and Bill
Who were flying in the sky

So they could look down on us
And watch us cry
While Public Officials gave us permission to die

After revealing our life
Out of context in Failing City
The story was never pretty

They embarrassed whoever they could
By putting their file so confidential
On the Net

CULTURAL GENOCIDE: Glue and Spy Included

Some victims lost their joy of life
Though they were not dead yet
Felt they had nothing of value to give

Were told suicide was the only way

To deny this truth
Jethro and Bill said
One must be sick in the head

For they knew how to play the game;
The power to break another person's mind
The best job in town;

To intrude in someone's personal space
Was the domain of the Parties
In charge and quite large

Manufactured words to create despair
Demoralization
A hurt sensation

For the abandoned generation

So intense
And so experimental
And always so impersonally personal.

The job of the Surveillance Men
Jethro and Bill
Were looking down at us, from the air.

Without a care
To tear one off
Right off their feet

When Puffy lost his job
Jethro and Bill were given this role
And the means was called mind control

CULTURAL GENOCIDE: Glue and Spy Included

Sometimes they wore Burghas
To hide their identity
But their shiny boots

And gun on hip
Gave them away
While we; the unbroken

And apologized in the usual way

We had been looking down
Saw those shiny boots and gun on hip
One more time again.

THE END

Produced by S.E. McKenzie Productions
First Print Edition June 2015

Enquiries: 1(778)992-2453
Mailing Address:
S. E. McKenzie Productions
168 B 5ᵗʰ St.
Courtenay, BC
V9N 1J4

Email Address:
messidartha@aol.com

http://www.amazon.com/SarahMcKenzie/e/B00H9RWX48/ref=ntt
_dp_epwbk_0

www.ingramcontent.com/pod-product-compliance
Lightning Source LLC
Chambersburg PA
CBHW070640030426
42337CB00020B/4099